# Cultural Traditions in

# Ghana

Joan Marie Galat

Crabtree Publishing Company
www.crabtreebooks.com

# Crabtree Publishing Company
## www.crabtreebooks.com

*For Doogutey Yamoi and Wapoo Kpelle, friends in Ghana*

**Author:** Joan Marie Galat

**Publishing plan research and development:**
Reagan Miller

**Editorial director:** Kathy Middleton

**Editor:** Janine Deschenes

**Proofreader:** Wendy Scavuzzo

**Photo research:** Abigail Smith

**Designer:** Abigail Smith

**Production coordinator and prepress technician:**
Abigail Smith

**Print coordinator:** Margaret Amy Salter

**Cover:** The arch of Independence at Independence Square in Accra (top, background); Ghanaian children play in the fields (middle); traditional Ghanaian musicians playing drums (middle right); dirt road in Ghana (bottom); traditional Ghanaian fufu dish (bottom left)

**Title page:** A dancer in traditional clothing

**Photographs:**
**Alamy:** Chuck Bigger, p7; Marion Kaplan. p9; Robert Burch, p11 (top); World Religions Photo Library, p14; Simon Rawles, p18; Thomas Cockrem, p24; Black Star, pp26, 27; robertharding p28 (inset); USAID, p29
**Getty Images:** Harry Hook, p5 (top); peeterv, p13 (bottom); Brian D Cruickshank, p15; CRISTINA ALDEHUELA, p23; Ariadne Van Zandbergen, p31 (top)
**iStock:** Snyderdf, p20
**Shutterstock:** © Anton_Ivanov, title page, Cover (bottom right), (boy and girl), pp6 (right), 8 (bottom left), 17, 19, 22, ; © Sura Nualpradid, pp6 (left), 31 (bottom); © Felix Lipov, Cover (bkgd)
**Wikimedia Commons:** Stug Nygaard, p4 (bottom); Brooklyn Museum, p 5 (bottom); DromoTetteh, p7 (inset); M_nunoo, p8 (inset); Kwameghana, p10 (right); Artbermiss, p16 (right); Anthony Cross, p25; Trees ForTheFuture, p28 (bkgd); Akiwumi, p30; Antoshananarivo, p30 (inset)

All other images by Shutterstock

### Library and Archives Canada Cataloguing in Publication

Galat, Joan Marie, 1963-, author
    Cultural traditions in Ghana / Joan Marie Galat.

(Cultural traditions in my world)
Includes index.
Issued in print and electronic formats.
ISBN 978-0-7787-8095-3 (hardcover).--
ISBN 978-0-7787-8103-5 (softcover).--
ISBN 978-1-4271-1950-6 (HTML)

    1. Holidays--Ghana--Juvenile literature. 2. Festivals--Ghana--Juvenile literature. 3. Ghana--Social life and customs--Juvenile literature. I. Title. II. Series: Cultural traditions in my world

GT4889.G4G35 2017      j394.269667      C2017-903511-8
                                             C2017-903512-6

### Library of Congress Cataloging-in-Publication Data

Names: Galat, Joan Marie, 1963- author.
Title: Cultural traditions in Ghana / Joan Marie Galat.
Description: New York, New York : Crabtree Publishing, 2018.
Series: Cultural traditions in my world | Includes index. | Audience: Age 5-8 | Audience: Grade K to 3.
Identifiers: LCCN 2017024404 (print) | LCCN 2017027910 (ebook) | ISBN 9781427119506 (Electronic HTML) | ISBN 9780778780953 (reinforced library binding) | ISBN 9780778781035 (pbk.)
Subjects: LCSH: Festivals--Ghana--Juveniel literature. | Ghana--Social life and customs--Juvenile literature.
Classification: LCC GT4889.G4 (ebook) | LCC GT4889.G4 G35 2018 (print) | DDC 394.269667--dc23
LC record available at https://lccn.loc.gov/2017024404

## Crabtree Publishing Company
www.crabtreebooks.com      1-800-387-7650

Printed in Canada/082017/EF20170629

**Published in Canada**
**Crabtree Publishing**
616 Welland Ave.
St. Catharines, ON
L2M 5V6

**Published in the United States**
**Crabtree Publishing**
PMB 59051
350 Fifth Avenue, 59th Floor
New York, New York 10118

**Published in the United Kingdom**
**Crabtree Publishing**
Maritime House
Basin Road North, Hove
BN41 1WR

**Published in Australia**
**Crabtree Publishing**
3 Charles Street
Coburg North
VIC 3058

# Contents

Welcome to Ghana . . . . . . . . . . . . . . 4

Naming Day . . . . . . . . . . . . . . . . . . 6

Birthdays . . . . . . . . . . . . . . . . . . . 8

New Year . . . . . . . . . . . . . . . . . . . 10

Independence Day . . . . . . . . . . . . . . 12

Religious Celebrations . . . . . . . . . . 14

National Celebrations . . . . . . . . . 18

Republic Day and Founder's Day. . . 20

Festivals All Year . . . . . . . . . . . . . 22

Homowo Festival . . . . . . . . . . . . . 24

Fetu Afahya and Odwira Festival . . . 26

Farmer's Day . . . . . . . . . . . . . . . . 28

Christmas and Boxing Day . . . . . . . 30

Glossary and Index . . . . . . . . . . . . 32

# Welcome to Ghana

More than 27 million people live in the **Republic** of Ghana, a warm country in western Africa. Ghana has a diverse culture of 50 different **ethnic** groups. Each has its own customs and languages, but English is the country's official language. Almost half of the population belongs to an ethnic group called the Akan.

BURKINA FASO

BENIN

**GHANA**

CÔTE D'IVOIRE

TOGO

ACCRA

*Gulf of Guinea*

Much of Ghana's land is made up of savannas, or low grasslands. Diverse animals, such as elephants and monkeys, live there.

4

Cultural **traditions** in Ghana are colorful! People may practice **Christianity, Islam,** or traditional religions. Relationships are important, and families like to celebrate special occasions together. National holidays, festivals, and religious days are recognized with food, music, dancing, and traditional clothing. Ghanaians are proud of their country's traditions and **independence**.

Fishing boats rest in this harbor in Accra, Ghana's capital city. Around 4 million people live there.

The Sankofa bird is an important symbol to the Akan people. Its head faces backward, reminding people that the past is a guide to the future.

5

# Naming Day

A child born in Ghana is kept inside for seven days to protect them from harm. After seven days, an "outdooring" ceremony is held to celebrate the child's birth and give the child a name. An Akan child is given three to four names. At the ceremony, the father, or an elder in the community, calls out the child's name and guests repeat the name out loud.

**Did You Know?**
Traditionally, Akan children are given first names based on the day of the week that they were born.

**For girls:**
Monday – Adwoa
Tuesday – Abena
Wednesday – Akua
Thursday – Yaa
Friday – Afua
Saturday – Ama
Sunday – Akosua

**For boys:**
Monday – Kwadwo
Tuesday – Kwabena
Wednesday – Kwaku
Thursday – Yaw
Friday – Kofi
Saturday – Kwame
Sunday – Kwasi

Friends and relatives give the baby gifts, such as money or jewelry. Everyone enjoys dancing and feasting. To prepare for naming days, older relatives teach younger family members to cook traditional foods, such as *kenkey*—**fermented** cornmeal wrapped in corn husks or plantain leaves.

**Did You Know?**
Ghanaians always eat food, such as kenkey, with their right hand.

Preparing food together is an important tradition for families in Ghana.

# Birthdays

Each ethnic group has its own birthday traditions, but eating *oto* for breakfast on one's birthday is a common tradition across Ghana. Oto is made of mashed yam and an onion-flavored liquid. It is often served with boiled eggs.

Yams—the largest ingredient in oto—are an important part of the Ghanaian diet.

**Did You Know?**
Family, friends, and neighbors often eat oto together, from one large dish.

Friends and family in Ghana spend time together to celebrate a birthday. Celebrations may include a birthday cake, soda, and *ampe*—a popular game that can be played with two people or in teams. When two play, a leader is chosen and both players jump in the air and clap twice. Each player puts one foot forward when landing. If both put the same foot forward, the leader gets a point. If the other player puts a different foot forward, that player becomes the leader.

Another popular game in Ghana is called *oware*. It is a traditional strategy game played between two people. Often, entire communities join in!

# New Year

Ghanaians welcome the New Year with parades, singing, and all kinds of dance and music, including drumming. They may wear colorful clothing to celebrate. People wish one another "Happy New Year" in English, and children often receive a gift. Public events are held with **durbars** of chiefs, or leaders, and queen mothers. Queen mothers are wise women who are trusted to give advice.

Each color on traditional Ghanaian clothing has a special meaning. For example, green means renewal, and blue represents a pure spirit.

Christians may also go to a religious service. Similar to other parts of the world, New Year's Eve may include a street carnival and fireworks. Ghanaians near the coast may go to a beach party that starts during the day, and includes a bonfire and dancing on the beach.

Ghanaians wear colorful clothing and walk on stilts during a New Year parade in Accra.

# Independence Day

For many years, Ghana was ruled over by Britain. On March 6, 1957, Kwame Nkrumah, Ghana's first president, led Ghana to become one of the first independent African countries. Now, March 6 is Independence Day. The celebration begins with music and speeches the night before Independence Day. Across the country, flags are raised and the national anthem is sung.

The Independence Arch in Accra (below) commemorates Ghanaian independence.

AD 1957

FREEDOM AND JUSTICE·

In Accra, many thousands of people gather at Black Star Square, also called Independence Square. Roads are closed for a parade with music, dancing, and marching military and police officers. People wave flags and some even paint their faces green, red, and yellow—the color of Ghana's flag.

The Eternal Flame of African Liberation burns in Black Star Square in this lamp. Liberation means freedom.

The Ghanaian army lines up in Black Star Square for an Independence Day parade.

# Religious Celebrations

Many people in Ghana enjoy national religious holidays. For Christians, Good Friday and Easter honor the death and **resurrection** of Jesus Christ. People may go to church on these days and celebrate Easter by visiting a beach or enjoying a picnic. Easter Monday is also an official holiday.

Palm Sunday is a Christian holiday celebrated the Sunday before Easter. Below, Ghanaians carry palm leaves through the town of Winneba.

On Good Friday, Christians do not eat meat. A few days later, Easter is celebrated with a feast. A special meal might include stews made with vegetables, fish, or meat. A goat or lamb may be roasted. Almost all meals include *fufu*. Spices such as cayenne pepper, curry, and chili peppers give Ghanaian food a strong taste.

Fufu is made of yams, plantains, or cassava. These are plant-based foods popular in Ghana. They are mixed with water into a soft dough.

**Muslim** Ghanaians take part in Ramadan—a period of 30 days of **fasting** when people only eat after sunset and before sunrise. Ramadan ends with a celebration called Eid al-Fitr—the Feast of Ramadan. During this special celebration, Muslim Ghanaians share food with friends and family, and children may receive gifts.

Muslim Ghanaians, such as these brothers, wear special clothing to celebrate Eid al-Fitr.

About one half of Ghanaians are Christian, and one fifth are Muslim. Some Ghanaians also practice traditional religions. They believe that they are connected to their ancestors, spirits or souls of the dead, and God—called *Nyame* in Akan.

This symbol represents Nyame, or God, in the Akan religion.

**Did You Know?**
Funerals are very important in Ghanaian culture. They are a way to celebrate the person who has died. These women wear traditional red-and-black funeral clothing, and perform a song.

# National Celebrations

Like many countries, Ghana has set aside a special day to honor workers. Celebrated on May 1, Labor Day is also called May Day. A national parade with colorful floats is held, and most people enjoy a day off work. Labor **unions** give awards to their best workers.

This woman works hard to harvest cocoa beans. Ghana is one of the biggest cocoa producers in the world.

Ghanaians enjoy another holiday on May 25, called African Unity Day or Africa Day. May 25 is the date that the Organisation of African Unity (OAU) was formed. On this day, people promote African unity. They encourage everyone to work together to build a safe Africa that gives everyone opportunities.

The African Union was formed in 2001. It creates cooperation between African countries. This is its symbol.

**Did You Know?** Drumming is part of almost every special occasion in Ghana.

# Republic Day and Founder's Day

Ghana became a republic—a nation with its own elected government—just over 60 years ago. Republic Day is celebrated on the day the Republic of Ghana was formed, on July 1, 1960. Along the coast, many people attend festive beach parties.

**Did You Know?**
Ghanaians may celebrate the nation's birthday by wearing the flag design or its colors. Red represents the blood of those who died for independence. Gold stands for Ghana's mineral wealth, and green is for its forests.

Founder's Day, on September 21, celebrates Kwame Nkrumah's birthday. He led Ghana to independence in 1957 and helped found the Republic of Ghana in 1960. On Founder's Day, people enjoy a day off work. The armed forces march in a parade, and raise the Ghana and African Union flags.

On Founder's Day, Ghanaians may visit this memorial of Kwame Nkrumah in Accra (below). The former president is buried there.

# Festivals All Year

People in Ghana love to have fun. A celebration occurs somewhere in the country almost every week. People join one another to sing, drum, and dance. They eat traditional foods and wear clothes made from traditional cloths, such as the brightly colored and patterned *kente*. Priests and chiefs lead **rituals**, and villagers take part in the durbar.

These children are performing traditional Ghanaian dances. They wear jewelry all over their bodies.

Seasonal festivals often celebrate the harvest and take the form of thanksgiving for good crops. One of the oldest is the Aboakyer Festival, also called the deer-catching festival. Two groups dress in traditional battle clothes and try to be the first to capture a live deer.

In the town of Winneba, hunters parade through the street after hunting a deer during the Aboakyer Festival.

# Homowo Festival

The Homowo Festival is a month-long corn harvest festival in Southern Ghana. It is celebrated by the Ga people. **Oral stories** say long ago, a spoiled **millet** crop caused the Ga people to go hungry. They planted corn to save themselves, then celebrated by making fun of hunger. The festival is named after the word homowo, which means, "hooting at hunger."

Large crowds of people dressed in traditional colors and clothing parade the streets during the Homowo Festival.

People return to their family homes for the festival, which usually begins in late July or early August. In some places, noise is not allowed before the event, to allow the gods to focus on making a good harvest. Steamed corn dough, called *kpekple*, is thrown on the ground for spirits and gods to eat. People feast, and hoot and yell to make fun of the famine.

**Did You Know?**
Oral storytelling is an important part of the Homowo Festival and is a tradition in Ghana. The stories usually include jokes, riddles, singing, or dancing.

# Fetu Afahya and Odwira Festival

The Fetu Afahye is an exciting Akan festival that celebrates the yam harvest and Cape Coast chiefs. On the first Saturday of September, people pack the streets to watch as the chiefs are carried by on fancy chairs, as shown below. Dancers move to the sound of drums and songs about the past.

There are multiple festivals dedicated to yam harvests in Ghana.

The weeklong Odwira Festival shows thanks for the yam harvest, too. It also honors those who died in the past year. Priests clean away evil spirits and chiefs lead a parade. Feasts are held on the Thursday, while Friday includes a great durbar and gifts for the spirits of the ancestors. Held in September or October, the festival celebrates the Akan New Year.

# Farmer's Day

In the 1980s, a drought in Ghana caused a poor harvest. A drought is a long period without rain. It caused many people to go hungry. Finally, rain fell from the sky. The drought reminded Ghanaians of the important work farmers do: grow the food people need to live. Farmer's Day, celebrated on the first Friday in December, became an official day to thank farmers for their work.

**Did You Know?**
People in Ghana may carry baskets of food, buckets of water, and other objects on their heads.

Each year, one person is named Ghana's National Best Farmer. Top farmers are invited to Accra to see the sights, visit the president, and enjoy fancy meals. On Farmer's Day, they are honored with prizes. The National Best Farmer receives the best prize, and last year's winner gives the new Best Farmer a **ceremonial** sword.

Many Ghanaian people rely on farming for their daily food. These women and children are collecting peas.

# Christmas and Boxing Day

Most Ghanaians celebrate Christmas. Christians honor the birth of Jesus by attending a church service. Everyone visits family and friends. Gift-giving is not common, but children may be given gifts, and told they are from Father Christmas. A special meal may include stew made with goat, chicken, or guinea fowl, which is a type of bird. Ghanaians may also eat peanut soup, or a soup made from snails.

**Did You Know?** Ghana has the world's largest snails! They can weigh as much as a baseball.

In the city of Takoradi, a carnival is held on Christmas. People dress in colorful costumes, as shown above, and parade in the streets.

Boxing Day, on December 26, is a tradition left from British rule. The holiday may be spent visiting family and friends. When Akan people meet, they say "*Afishapa*," (ah-fih-SHOP-uh) which means "Merry Christmas and Happy New Year."

# Glossary

**ceremonial** Formal or official; relating to a ceremony

**Christianity** A religion that follows the teachings of Jesus Christ, whom they believe to be the Son of God

**durbar** A parade in which everyone follows the chief or leader through the streets to the festival

**ethnic** Relating to a group with a common background or culture

**fasting** To not eat food

**fermented** The breaking down of a substance over time, usually becoming softer or growing some bacteria

**independence** Ability to rule itself

**Islam** A religion that follows one God through the teachings of the prophet Muhammad

**millet** An edible seeded grass

**Muslim** A person who practices Islam

**oral stories** Spoken stories; not written

**republic** A country or state in which citizens vote for their leaders

**resurrection** To come back from the dead

**rituals** Ceremonies that follow a certain tradition or order

**traditions** A group's beliefs or customs

**unions** Groups of workers who work together to protect and improve their rights as workers

# Index

Accra 4, 5, 11, 12, 13, 29
African Union 19, 21
Akan people 4, 5, 6, 17, 23, 26, 27, 31
ampe 9
Christians 5, 11, 14, 15, 16, 30
dancing 5, 7, 10, 11, 13, 22, 25, 26
drumming 10, 19, 22, 26, 27
durbar 10, 22, 27
farming 18, 28, 29
fasting 16
flags 12, 13, 20, w 21
foods 7, 8, 15, 16, 22, 28, 29, 30
fufu 15
Independence 5, 12, 13, 20, 21
Islam 5, 16
kenkey 22
oto 8
parades 10, 22, 13, 18, 21, 22, 23, 24, 27, 31
republic 4, 12, 20
stories 24, 25
traditions 5, 6, 7, 8, 17, 22, 23, 24, 25, 26, 31
yams 8, 15, 26, 27